**ANCHOR BOOKS**

A POETRY PATCHWORK

Edited by

Rachael Radford

First published in Great Britain in 2003 by
ANCHOR BOOKS
Remus House,
Coltsfoot Drive,
Peterborough, PE2 9JX
Telephone (01733) 898102

HB ISBN 1 84418 076 X
SB ISBN 1 84418 077 8

FOREWORD

Poetry has become more and more popular over recent years - with people choosing to write poems in order to unchain feelings and emotions. This special anthology of poetry, *A Poetry Patchwork,* acts as a platform for both new and established writers to share their work with a wider audience.

The chosen subjects of the writers vary but they use their creativity to the full in order to share views and pass on thought-provoking messages. The poems are easy to relate to and encouraging to read, offering engaging entertainment to their reader.

This delightful collection is sure to win your heart, making it a companion for life and perhaps even earning that favourite little spot upon your bookshelf.

Rachael Radford
Editor

Sundays Mystery Tour
On Page 80

Written by:-
    Susan Carole Roberts

CONTENTS

GOING FORWARD

Surf the Earth in a minute,
Hear the news as it happens,
Send a letter in a flash,
Buy with plastic cards not cash.
Mobile phones with digit tones,
Satellite dishes stuck on homes,
Weather pictures viewed from space,
Telescopes see comets race.
Data at the touch of key,
Living with technology.

Linda Knight

MUSH

I see the truest part of your soul,
Most people miss the best part,
They see the joker of your personality,
They don't see the beauty in your heart.

Granted there are still some places,
That I have yet to open within your mind,
I look forward to more discoveries about the real you,
And what more of your soul I find.

What can I say about you,
That you don't already see in the mirror's reflection?
You're sweet, shy and basically you're just you,
Glowing with love and consideration.

Kimberly Harries

THE HANDS OF TIME

If I could turn back the hands of time,
I would be everything my parents wanted;
I would strive hard at school for the results I needed,
I would be closer to my sister who I never really hated.

If I could turn back the hands of time,
I would work hard for the money I wanted;
I would not argue with my parents about clothes I needed
I would be kinder to my cousin because we're related.

If I could turn back the hands of time,
I would listen to my parents about the boys I dated;
I would not stay out late so their fears are abated,
I would be the daughter they were proud to be related.

If I could turn back the hands of time,
I would listen to my mother's fears of dying;
I would tell her I loved her with feelings abounding,
I would be there for her after all the crying.

If I could turn back the hands of time,
I would be beside her in her final hours;
I would hold her closely to show her how much I cared,
I would appreciate the love and wisdom she shared.

Janet Gardner

THE DENTIST'S CHAIR

I don't believe, I'm here today,
Third time lucky, or so they say.
Sitting in this, the dentist's chair,
I'm uptight . . . she doesn't care.

There she stands, the drill in her hand,
Looking quite powerful, feeling grand.

But unknown to her . . . she won't scare me,
I'll suffer the pain, and pay the fee.
Then out of this place, on my way,
That bitch of a dentist will have to stay.

Forever looking . . . down a person's throat,
Please forgive me . . . but I need to gloat.

Because in time . . . and eventually,
No more pain, will she inflict upon me.
My teeth they'll fall out, one by one,
So lady dentist . . . another sucker is gone.

But, you'll still be there without a care,
May you RIP . . . in your own, dentist's chair . . .

Pensioner Pam

WARWICKSHIRE IN MAY

As a child I wandered
Through many an endless day
Along the lanes of Warwickshire
In the pleasant month of May.

The green month, the clean month,
The month of cuckoo call.
The month that heralds summer,
The sweetest month of all.

The sky seemed always perfect,
An endless stretch of blue,
As I walked the lanes of Warwickshire
The whole month through.

The green month, the clean month,
The month of cuckoo call.
The month that heralds summer,
The sweetest month of all.

The birds were always busy
With the young they had to rear
In their nests along the hedgerows
In this best month of the year.

The green month, the clean month,
The month of cuckoo call.
The month that heralds summer,
The sweetest month of all.

In drifts so deep the may hung down,
And dressed the lanes in white.
The leafy lanes of Warwickshire,
A sweet and tranquil sight.

In the green month, the clean month,
The month of cuckoo call.
The month that heralds summer,
The sweetest month of all.

The violet hid beneath the hedge,
The buttercup shone gold.
The daisy starred the fields beyond,
And lambs played in the fold.

In the green month, the clean month,
The month of cuckoo call.
The month that heralds summer,
The sweetest month of all.

My feet were dusty in the lane
'Til there came a sudden shower.
Gentle rain from heaven
For that Warwickshire bower.

In the green month, the clean month,
The month of cuckoo call.
The month that heralds summer,
The sweetest month of all.

The woods I passed were cool and dim,
With a carpet laid out there.
The deepest blue amidst the green,
The bluebells sweet and fair.

The green month, the clean month,
The month of cuckoo call.
The month that heralds summer,
The sweetest month of all.

And cow parsley as fine as lace
Reached up to touch the may.
In the bridal lanes of Warwickshire
On each far-off childhood day.

The green month, the clean month,
The month of cuckoo call.
The month that heralds summer,
The sweetest month of all.

Frances Marie Cecelia Harvey

PAIN IN VAIN

Two more children, not going home again,
Their poor parents, all that pain,
How can people do such awful things,
Destroying innocence and love, that only childhood brings?
These dreadful crimes shock the nation,
People from every walk and station,
United in grief,
Shock, horror, disbelief.
Examples must surely be set,
As no one has found a deterrent yet.

Saying they are sick, just isn't true,
They know exactly what they do,
Bringing misery and grief to everyone,
Is their warped idea of fun,
Please stop this happening again,
Or these dear children, are dying in vain.

Maureen Arnold

DADDY PUTS HIS FOOT IN IT!

I had the first shower yesterday.
I don't know why that was.
Daddy's usually first up
But my brain began to buzz.

I had a very quick shower,
Then stood on the vinyl floor.
The water all dripped off me
As I stood near the bathroom door.

It was then my daddy surfaced,
Sleepy head still in a muddle.
He put his left foot forward
And stepped right in *my* puddle.

His left foot skidded forwards
As he fell down with a loud crash.
He just lay there, flat on his back,
So for Mummy I had to dash.

'Quick, Daddy's fallen over!
He's lying in a heap!'
Mummy opened up one eye,
(Because *she* was still asleep.)

My daddy wasn't moving,
Though he *did* begin to moan.
'Get up! Get up! Stop messing about!'
'I'm not!' my daddy did groan.

'Have you broken anything?'
'I think I've hurt my shoulder.'
'Well, see if you can stand up.
You should be more careful when you're older!'

Timothy Jasper

LIFE'S STRUGGLES

When we were all simply children,
Who knew no better and cared even less.
The system controlled our behaviour and desires,
Defined by others - involved in our past.

Then as youths we seek rebellion and adventure,
With a thrill each moment and in every event.
No thought to the future - or others,
No worries beyond our own discontent.

And as time moves on and on,
We evolve to look to the familiar.
Hoping for family life and structure,
With all its supposed security to entrance.

Gary J Finlay

PICTURES IN THE CLOUDS

Watching clouds go floating by
In a summer's deep blue sky
Is that a dragon I can see?
And an angel looking down on me
Maps of different places
Men with beards, and cherubs faces
Oh what pictures clouds provide
As quietly overhead they glide.

D L Critchley

L'AAL RATTY

Have you heard about L'aal Ratty, the Eskdale Special Train -
It rattles up the dale and down again;
Steaming along beside the fell, and through the shady wood,
Stopping for breath at the stations, Eskdale Green and Irton Road;
And when it reaches Dalegarth, eight miles up the dale,
A turntable turns the engine, while the passengers tell their tale!

You pick it up at Ravenglass, and choose a corner seat,
(Either in a covered car, or open to the heat),
The engine's getting steamed up, it may be Irt or Mite,
A miniature steam engine, with paint and brasses bright -
The seats are full, the whistle blows! . . .
All waves and cheering, off she goes!

Steaming along the narrow gauge line, L'aal Ratty's quite a sight,
Weaving between the bracken fronds, and foxgloves pink and white;
In spring, folk reach for the bluebells, in summer they look for nuts,
While others reach for their plastic hoods, as the wind puffs
                                                    back the smuts!
People lean over the bridges, to wave to their friends below -
See, how excitement and mountain air is making their faces glow!

Oh, some will use L'aal Ratty just to get from A to B -
They're kitted up with boots and ropes, and knapsacks on their knee;
Well, they can go a-climbing, and many a view they'll see,
But a gay little puffing steam train is adventure enough for me!

Mary Dimond

HUMOROUS TALE

A man made a wish
To be a big fish
And the wish came true
He was swallowed by a whale
Which is the end of the tale
That's how the whale became blue.

Violetta Jean Ferguson

IT'S JUST A BUNCH OF ROSES

One dull day, I asked my wife, 'Honey, what do you expect from me?'
She replied briefly, 'For you to earn the money, so I can buy
food for the tea.'
'Oh!' I retorted, 'I now know my place in our married life,
Except, I thought I was here to love, protect and cherish
my beautiful wife.'
She then rather positively and abruptly - if I may add, just went
to pieces and snapped.
'Well, my dear husband, I think you've got it very wrong, I am
just your servant and I feel trapped!'
Then she stormed out the room and a long silence was between
us all through the night
And I thought all along our loving togetherness, was going to be alright.
So, next day, after work, I went to the florist to buy her a
bunch of roses to patch the argument up.
Only to get back home to find a note on the table beside my
favourite coffee cup.
The words on it simply read.
'Gone to live with my mother instead.'
I sat down in that kitchen, not on a chair but the floor.
Coming to terms with the fact, she didn't love me anymore.
Pondered and analysed over every possible reason
Perhaps it was the time of the anti-mating season.
However, I came to a final decision on what I was going to do
Decided, I simply didn't have a bloomin' clue.
Picked up the car keys and said 'Oh damn it.'
Then threw the ruddy flowers into the waste disposal bucket.
Just so sorry the end bit there sounded like I was finally in my glory
Truthfully? Well, I was hurting and now so glad that
you've read my story.
As through many years you probably have seen
Mine's is not the only marriage break up there's ever been.
Unfortunately, there's no bandage or plaster to mend a broken heart.
Only those others out there, that can give comfort, relief and
well, that's a good start.

Next time, I won't be so eager to get a wedding band on a lady's finger
Cos, it's don't come with a guarantee that she will linger.
Now I am going to find a swell, bachelor pad
And simply reflect on the marriage that I once had.

Margo Baxter

HOME SWEET HOME PLUS OUR KITCHEN

Home is where the heart is and that's a fact
It's May and Tom's said kitchen that's that
Pride in it you can bet on that no fret
More so now that daughter Our Pat
Plus our son-in-law Our Dave no regret
Of having a new kitchen unit to cook
By golly you are welcome to have a look
There was more pride in the work carried out
You only had to look upon Our Pat's face
As she painted the doors around the place
Was just like an artist viewing his work
Say of a master piece in his case
Before Pat and Dave started to wipe off the dirt
Sandpaper firstly get off the shine good
Dave had to wash the walls down know he should
Jersey Cream, the emulsion was named OK
You bet we Pat's mum and me Pop no words to say
No praise bigger enough for us two no way
In our old lives they both have a part to play
They did it all for love we love them too we say
Our thanks go out to them both Mum and Dad, Tom and May.

T Sexton

THE TRULY AWESOME PONG

One lovely Easter Sunday, when I was ten plus three,
We got an invitation to attend my aunt's for tea.
I wasn't very happy: I did not want to go:
I was spotty, plump and anxious:
It was a teenage thing, you know.
But choice, there was not any,
My parents dragged me along
And that's when I encountered this truly awesome pong.
We sat around the table and Aunty passed the plates,
'Just help yourselves, my dears,' she said,
So we chobbled, chewed and ate.
Then the atmosphere began to change as a smell began to rise,
Our faces turned from pink to red and we all cast down our eyes.
Aunty did excuse herself and promptly left the room,
Abandoning the rest of us to breathe the noxious fumes.
'Poor old Aunty Ivy,' said my father with a grin.
'It must have been the sausage rolls,' my mother butted in.
Then back came flustered Aunty with a can of scented peach,
She lifted up the tablecloth and squirted underneath.
'You smelly dog!' she shouted, 'We've got visitors today,'
She aimed the spout at a hairy lump and then began to spray.
From underneath his hiding place skulked old Aunt Ivy's dog
We now felt very bad for thinking Aunty made the pong.
And so we blamed the baffled hound for making the gruesome smell,
But I know who it really was -
And I'm not going to tell.

Carole Wale

MUSA

The hours and days are longer
The nights I never sleep
I lay there listening, waiting
My heart it skips a beat.

You're always in my thoughts
And through my waking day
All my thinking's just of you
You're never far away.

And though I keep it silent
And you may never know
I wish that I could shout it out
How much I love you so!

Susan Stark

MISTER LATE

Can you tell me Johnny Ray
Why you're late for work every single day?
You have such a black
Way of seeing things Jack
I arrive early for the next morning I say!

Joan Wylde

MY PALADIN

You were my paladin,
A ballad in my heart.
But you fell from grace,
When you spurned me,
Turned on me,
Full of revenge,
Trying to avenge,
The beauty of my dreams.
They were of such importance,
They consumed me immense,
My candles burning sweet incense,
Now look at the true consequence,
For all you speak of is just nonsense.
When you offer me a present, I can see,
It's tied with ribbons of trickery.
You handed me a smile,
Like a sunny day,
Then rolled the rain clouds to me,
Every day.
You were my paladin,
A ballad in my heart.
With deep intense,
In confidence,
I trusted you,
It was not sense.
Now I am in reticence.
You were my paladin,
A ballad in my heart,
My hero now fallen.

Carol Ann Darling

THE BEST MEDICINE HUMOUR

One day,
Minnie and Jimmy,
Went for a ride,
They jumped over a fence,
So big and wide,
Minnie let out a scream,
As she fell into a stream,
At the other side,
And got wet through,
Jimmy looked back and said 'Neigh, neigh.'
Then galloped away.

Jane Milthorp

SUPPLE SUCKLE, SUBTLE SUCKERS

One can puff a cloud of dirty smoke
Into a stranger's eyes,
But, do not breastfeed in public
We are now too sanitised.

You can smell of stale tobacco
In a shop or on the bus,
But, do not feed baby naturally
Such sights now cause a fuss.

It is so 'grown up' to suck a comforter
In any place you wish,
But, do not suckle baby here
Such sights are not so swish.

The harm caused by your habit
You do not care about,
Or the goodness and the beauty
When a mother's breast is out.

Did I see you, the other day
'Men's' magazines in hand?
You ogled every picture
Every tit-pic on the stand.

Cigarette sucking selfishness
Leaves litter, fumes and muck,
Thank God for natural feeding
I know which I would rather suck!

Joseph McGarraghy

SICK AS A DOG

She was sick at the bottom of the garden,
The day she ate a frog.
Her pooh was all green and grungy,
Like a monster from a fictional bog.

She was sick in the street down a grid,
The day she ate a mouse.
She went home feeling pretty lousy,
And was sick all over the house.

She was sick in the school playground,
The day she ate a spider,
Whether she'd have diarrhoea,
Eating flies had been the decider.

She was sick all the way down the staircase,
The day she ate on some soap.
Her pooh came out with some bubbles next day,
And looked similar to soap-on-a-rope.

She was sick all over the sofa,
The day she ate puss from a blister.
No wonder she's always as sick as a dog,
She'll eat anything, my two-year-old sister!

Nigel Stanley

UNTITLED

There was a poor boy named Noah
Who lived in a village in Goa
He had a pet boa
Which he kept in a round basket.

One day at the zoo, it escaped from its casket,
Noah cried boo hoo!
Just then he had to go to the loo
And there Noah found not one boa
But two.

Jason Wilde

THE STREAKER

Now you are getting older,
And feeling weaker and weaker,
Take up indoor bowling,
You might see that buxom streaker.

It won't happen every week,
But if you're very keen,
You'll crouch to deliver the winning shot,
And see her bouncing down the green.

This may make you go all wobbly
And drop the winning shot,
But at least you will get an eyeful
Of all the wobbly bits she's got!

Margaret East

PC BLEACH

(To my good friend JcMG
a wizard with software)

A computer owner's nightmare, an operator's pox,
Placed inside the software of my Compaq tower box.
Sadistic hacking terrorists so small you cannot see,
After all the work you've done so hard, they've taken the PC.
To purge and start all over again, your files at such a loss,
Miles and miles of code commands inside your MS Dos.
Inside the words, a virus cure just like the advert said,
New improved MS Dos kills all your virus dead.
These novel ways of keeping clear a precious software breach,
A disinfecting program, the perfect PC bleach.

A Bray

CHRISTMAS LONG AGO

I opened my eyes, on Christmas Day and there I see
A stripy pillow of things for me
An orange, a pear and Mommy look
My bestest favourite Rupert book
Pencils colourful, wrapped in brown paper
Oh Mommy thank you so much, I'll play with them later
There are Blue Bird Toffees, in a shiny tin
And a soft fluffy toy with a silly grin
Chocolates wrapped up in a shiny box of gold
I'm going downstairs now, I'm getting cold
Daddy look at all my wonderful things
Wrapped up in pretty paper and silver string
Today has been the most bestest time
Mommy and Daddy you made everything just fine
Father Christmas thank you so, I've had a super, super day
I'm only four years old, it's been difficult to say
Thank you.

Ann Hathaway

AUTOMATION

Today I saw the ultimate,
A wheelbarrow with its minder
Which dealt with its load
Deposited it, repeated its task
Again, again and again
And the minder walked alongside.

Muriel Reed

HALLOWE'EN REDUX

All morning and all afternoon they spent
creating guises weirdly stitched
from sheets and rags and painting masks
with holes cut out for goblin eyes
anticipating sugared treats to be amassed
in the spooky dark on that All Hallow's Eve.

Their parents warned of where small ghosts
and witches dare not wander. Explicitly
not cross the street to yonder where
old Nelly Storch that fateful night
across her porch had draped a rope
and thereon hung a sign which read
'Wet Paint
Young Ghosts Keep Off.'

Each wraith residing on the street knew
never to expect a treat from that one
so, as dark fell down they all trekked off
most joyously, some scared
but bold and spent the hours (least it is told)
in tricking and in treating, until at last
with bulging sacks, they all made tracks
back home, where sitting 'round they ate
their horde of pre-wrapped candy bars.

Next morning, so the story goes
when Nelly stepped out on her porch
alas, her slippered foot got stuck, quite fast
to its warped sticky boards and history
records some elves, most furtive on that
Hallowe'en, had struck to paint Miss Storch's porch
a bright and bilious shade of green.

Carol D Glover

NAME DROPPING

To represent your homeland on a trip across the sea,
To boast with pride of where ye' bide means more than most to me,
As ambassador of Scotland on my annual summer tour,
In a role I'm right at home with, even on a foreign shore.
With a wealth of which to choose from when promoting
                                        Scotland's fame,
So, by way of introduction, let me list below some names.

You'll have heard of William Wallace, Walter Scott and Robert Bruce?
Mary Stuart and her adversary John Knox.
James the sixth and first (of England, since united in a truce),
Plus a host of other, less distinguished Jocks.

I refer to Roy Magregor, Deacon Brodie, young Montrose,
Bonnie Charlie, Flo. McDonald and Argyll,
Not to mention Mary Slessor, Livingstone and such as those,
Robert Burns and later Arthur Conan Doyle.

Louis Stevenson is worthy, Logie-Baird deserves some praise,
The Ghillie brown and Alexander Graham rings a Bell,
See, I can't keep from name dropping when I'm in a foreign place,
And there's others which should 'go down' just as well.

Do you know of 'Johnny Walkers' have you heard of 'Langs Supreme?'
Pay attention to the 'Teachers' (For your info - 'Highland Cream)
'J & B' are well worth knowing, and as far as I can tell,
I have never yet regretted meeting blender 'Arthur Bell'.

With the 'Dewars' and the 'Ballantynes' both noted for good taste,
Yet the choice is wide and varied and should not be made in haste,
Then there's 'Crawfords' highly rated, for in fact it's got five stars,
And it can't be overstated, 'Chivas' dignifies most bars.

Two well known guys, 'Whyte & Mackays' are worthy of a
                                  mention on my list,
Like 'Mackinleys' and 'Macallans' a shot from each of
                                  these should not be missed.
'Matthew Gloags' not so familiar, 'though I've had him in my house'
A most popular Scots export, but at home he's know as 'Grouse'.

So, the moral of these verses and the reason that I boast,
To express my pride in Scotland in a simple, loyal toast.
When I'm in another country, when I cross another sea -
'To make damn sure, the dram I pour - makes Scotland proud of me.'

Derek Alexander

HUMOUR

This gardener, his name was Bill Baker,
Used to sleep on the beach in Jamaica.
While snoozing in bed
So a beachcomber said,
The crabs came and pinched his taters.

G Nicklin

No Me . . . No You

Now is the time
The time to fear,
The smell of death
Is uncomfortably near.

The world's getting old
So dirty too,
Some time in the future
There'll be no me . . . no you.

All it takes is for you to see
That the world needs help from us,
Take time to look, take time to notice
You don't need to cause a fuss.

The world needs help
So do the animals too,
Or else some time in the future
There'll be no me . . . no you.

Zoë Mitchell

My Dream

If I had a dream, what would it be?
My thoughts awake, surrounding me
Conveying feelings from my past
Strong feelings then that did not last.

My dream would be to never die
To flee this world but yet to fly
To oversee what has been done
And then begin what was begun.

A second time would bring new hope
A second start up life's long slope
A second view at all our woe
A second try, good to bestow.

As on a rock, good must be built
If built on sand, it turns to silt
The deeds begun must not be left
Or human souls will rot bereft

of hope. Their days will end
Without the peace that truth does send
So, dream, awake, be part of me
May my dulled eyes look inwardly.

May I deny what I was not
May I become one little spot
Of tireless time that leaves its mark
A gleaming light within the dark.

Death should not be a final step
But into truth it is the map
It shows the way, it guides anew
It brings us hope as truth we view.

My dream would be to never die
To flee this world but yet to fly
Above the fear, the wrong and lies
The jeers of men, their shouts and cries.

My death would be a place to start
The future drawn, the skill of art,
I'd chalk the lines of inner worth
And with it win my own rebirth.

The day is done, the morrow comes
I've lived my life, I've done my sums.
There was some good along the way,
'He spoke the truth,' I hear them say.

But do they know the inner lie
The life I've lead, my fear to die?
And so my dream must always be
To come again, another me.

Another chance to get it right
By chasing ogres through the night
Once banished, I am free to fly
Then only truth, will I espy.

Ruth Chignell-Stapleton

FRUITY FORTS

Oh, for a melody to croon,
Extolling virtues of the prune.
This fruity favourite though un-sung,
Internal problems, will unbung,
Sadly wrinkled, like wizened sage,
It looks the same, at any age,
Mark well the words written in this ballad,
Prunes grace a dish of any salad,
But flesh of flesh, and bone of bone
What on earth can one do with a used prune stone . . ?

Orange peel give me the pip (s)
As from my hand it deftly slips
I wouldn't this so much have minded,
If the spraying juice had not so blinded
My eyes, as supple thumbs insert,
Can this citrus really be inert . . ?
I have tried a knife, a saw, a spanner,
From now on, I'll stick to a banana.

Lew Park

The Financial Times

The doors open wide,
Commuters rush in!
They take up their seats,
And the chatter begins.

City gents, business men
Secretaries and staff
With one thing in common,
London!
Last stop.

Glancing through newspapers,
Reading their books,
Filling in crosswords
And checking the shares.

Others sit quietly,
And stare up ahead
Some fall asleep
They should be in bed.

And so to the station!
Or on to the tube
The train is left empty
With just papers behind!

Layers of newspapers
The Financial Times.

Anne Hyde

SONG AND DANCE WORDS

Choose some musical words for me
Pick them out and set them free.
Let me hear their special tune
As they sing or softly croon.
If you like to make words jazz
Use razzle-dazzle, razzmatazz.
Linger longer lullabies,
Make sleepy music in the skies.
Hocus-pocus, mumbo-jumbo
Chant out their magic as they go.
Hullabaloo loves to bellow
Brouhaha's a noisy fellow
Some words can dance upon the page
Using their writings as a stage.
Hear the rhythm of their beat
Setting off your dancing feet.
Tiptoe tapping without a care
And soft-shoe shuffles fill the air.
Rocking horses and cradles too
Suggest their rock 'n' roll to you.
Words like lovers, sweetheart, kiss
Sing out their happiness and bliss
By painting pictures in the mind
Musical magic's left behind.
Some words like to join their friends.
But it is up to you to choose
The song and dance words that you use.

Margaret Nixon

LIFE IS LIKE

'Life is like that!' the best man said
Halfway through his speech
'You just never-ever know, not at all,
The kind of girl you're going to meet.'

'Life is like that,' the best man said
After another glass of wine
Because he will always remember where they met
And where they were was not so fine.

'Life is like that,' the best man said
Who said there was nothing he could add at all
Just that he wanted them to be happy
And regret nothing at all.

Keith L Powell

ODE TO OUR BLUE BEACH

I

Today I'm in love
And my love is the sea,
She's asked me to share
Her bed so free -
I caught her waves
With laughing arms,
Her play was gentle,
She meant no harm.
I know she kissed me,
And that I replied.
Cradled we lay
In bliss of tide.
She smiled and beckoned
Me on and on,
I ceased to reckon
How far I'd gone.

After return into
            pristine sand,
Of our assiduously
            revamped strand.

II

I sent a smile
To the bunting on high
That flapped in the breeze
To woo passers-by,
Hurray! Now a toddler
Full of glee
Was making crab-like
For the sea.

Parents alert
Let him explore,
There's space for
Many more!

Veronica Ryecart

REGRETS

So many things I left unsaid,
The words remained inside my head.
Never knew quite what to say,
Feelings hidden, locked away
And now the chance has passed me by,
You've joined the angels up on high.
A gentle man, good friend to all.
Musical talents, I recall,
Your sense of humour, Yorkshire style,
Was guaranteed to bring a smile.
Sometimes as stubborn as a mule,
But definitely nobody's fool.
Such special qualities you had,
Oh how I loved you, dear old Dad
And if you're looking down on me,
Please set my guilty conscience free,
For I regret, with all my heart
Those thoughts which I did not impart.

Sue Mackenzie

HOLIDAY CARDS

Idyll of summer now has gone,
Yet still today,
Holiday cards to those alone
For ever stay.

They came from Finland's colder clime:
From sunny Spain.
From where the Indian temples chime,
Of long-lost reign.

National dress is shown with pride,
In colours bright.
And greetings from where e'er they bide,
Tho' far from sight.

So in the winter days ahead
Memories store!
Despite four walls, life is not dead,
There's still much more!

Ruth Shallard

STRANGERS ONE DAY

Two strangers met on a cold, wet day
Going about their business in their normal way
His eyes met hers, for just a short while
As her face became a bright beaming smile
Not knowing where to look or what to do
She tripped up the curb and lost her shoe
Trying to put it back on her foot so cold
That handsome man stood there tall and bold
Wow! She thought, what could this be?
Could it be love at last for me?
They talked together for an hour or so
The cold air by then, felt like a warm glow
Love was what the two had found for sure
No more emptiness or loneliness anymore
They met every day for the next fortnight
Everything went just perfectly right
He popped the question, will you be my wife
To have and to hold for the rest of my life?
Her answer was yes, without a doubt in her mind
For this man in her life was one of a kind
Never in her life would she ever let him go
And always for him she would let her love show
A happy end from the time when they first met
Two strangers on that day, being so cold and wet.

Vera M Seaman

RELEASE

I should have let my brain breathe
My mother said to me
So then she cut my hair quite short
And let my thoughtwaves free!

Barry Clist

UNTITLED

Why are we all here?
Who knows what they're doing?
Some people live in fear
Thinking where's it all leading?

For most, they have to work
The view of some is narrow
Many may only carry a smirk
While others fall into sorrow

Most have little time to think
Caring pittance for nature
They give each other a wink
Saying so what, about the future?

The world just carries on
Revolving into eternity
With only one mission
Not bowing to humanity

How much can the Earth stand
Resisting abuse from mankind?
Flames of destruction are fanned
By those with a small mind.

Jim Potter

SPIDER'S SONG

The woman across the street is baking humble pie,
and the guy two doors down is drinking his well dry.
I'm alone and wondering who the guilty really are,
because sometimes it just seems that life can be bizarre.
A few little words is all it takes, to start a web of sorrow,
and the spiders of this world won't think about tomorrow.
So people's lives get shattered by the wagging of a tongue,
then the gossips tune their art, and the spinning has begun.
Silent victims hear no words when the whispers start unfound,
backs are turned and secrets kept while the lies are passed around.
But defence is not an issue as this song has just one verse,
and those who gladly sing along don't take time to rehearse.
Some will learn those awful lines, and be brought down to their knees,
then they'll pray to the god of truth, who might ignore their pleas.
With luck, they find a champion, or a way to save the day,
then the spiders scurry off, as their web is blown away.
So words said in innocence can be twisted to sound wrong,
when no one reads between the lines of a spinning spider's song.

M M Graham

BEN

Dear old Ben, known him since I can't think when
To greet him, such a welcome he would give
He made our lives a joy to live
His kind eyes and handsome old face
A beautiful coat, and slow walking pace
No one could help but love his grace
And none can ever take his place
Now he is gone, but his memory will live
All the love and devotion he had to give
We his friends, can never forget
A beautiful old doggy, the best ever yet

C King

I'm Very Well Thank You

I'm as healthy and fit as can be,
There's nothing the matter with me,
Except when I talk I have a slight wheeze,
Sometimes there's a pain in both of my knees,
My memory's failing, my head's in a spin,
But I'm awfully well for the shape I am in.

There is nothing wrong, I've often heard said,
I wonder sometimes as I climb into bed,
My back now in spasm, my legs giving up,
My pills on the table in case I wake up,
As sleep over takes me, I say don't give in
You're awfully well for the shape you are in.

Long sleep is denied me, night after night,
Yet every morning I find I'm alright,
The stick that I use when up on my feet,
Hooks on the bedpost, next to my teeth,
My pulse gets erratic, my blood is too thin,
But I'm awfully well for the shape I am in.

I rise up quite early, the sky is still black,
To walk to the shops, and puff my way back,
It helps me each day to dust off my wits,
To pick up the paper and read the obits,
My name is still missing, I say with a grin,
I'm awfully well for the shape I am in.

The moral is this, as my tale I unfold,
For all of us pensioners feeling the cold,
Who know all our savings are finally spent,
And our get up and go, has got up and went,
Just stand up real tall and stick out your chin,
You're awfully well for the shape you are in.

K Townsley

WHOOPS!

The operation was proceeding well,
Anaesthetist and surgeon, both could tell,
But then the patient woke,
Critically she spoke.
Turned to each - to each accuse,
Not one of them would she excuse.
Struggling up, she managed to sit
And said with a scowl, 'You've missed a bit.'

They sent her home - she was discharged,
With hernia gone, but limb enlarged.
In fav'rite chair she sat,
Reviewing her habitat.
I know I'm a slow mover
Presented with a Hoover.
Some dust escaped - she had a fit,
'You lazy soul, you've missed a bit.'

To convalesce we went to Rome
And thereby missed the cold at home.
We went with naïve hope,
Perhaps to see the Pope
And in the Sistine Chapel
Michelangelo his art to dapple
Upward she gazed with eyes brightly lit
And gleefully cried, 'You've missed a bit.'

I've tried so hard to see the light,
Whate'er undertaken, to do it right.
Yet I feel there is something wrong,
Perhaps a different song.
What is adrift? In the rhyme or scan?
I'll put it right if I possibly can.
Ah now at last, I've mastered it
And know what's wrong, I've missed a bit!

Maurice Bailey

WHERE HAVE ALL THE BUSES GONE?
(With apologies to Bob Dylan)

Where have all the buses gone?
Long time coming.
Where have all the buses gone?
Long time ago.
Where have all the buses gone?
Gone to scrapheaps, every one.
When will they ever learn?
When will they ever learn?

Mary Hodson

The Chaotic Classroom

The teacher strode to the front of the classroom,
'Quiet!' he shrieked in a deafening boom.
This did not have the desired effect,
As still the pupils showed no respect.
Losing patience he continued with his chore,
'Shut up!' he cried in a loud roar.

The students had grown deaf to his pleading,
And persisted with their ritual feeding.
Lunchtime had come all to soon for Sir,
The morning seemingly gone in a blur.
'How dare you defy my wishes' he was restraining himself
from swearing
But his actions seemed as though he was far from caring.

'If the noise remains, the Headmaster will come!'
However the threat was not disturbing some.
True to his word the Head did appear,
Maybe sensing the teacher's fear,
He stood in the doorway amazed,
Viewing the chaos and looking a little phased.

The teacher bound over, apologising above the din, he cried,
The Head forgave him, saying he had tried,
'I'll take the situation from here' he declared,
The teacher resigned and simply stared.
Leaning next to the window, he watched the expert at toil,
But with the noise not subsiding, he was reaching the boil.

Both teachers stood together,
Seemingly reaching the end of their tether,
There they stayed talking for a short time,
Suddenly they executed their crime,
'Make more noise children!' came the teachers' yell,
. . . Silence . . . prevailed and they could hear the fire bell!

Ruth Morris

HAMPSHIRE HAUNTS

Into the New Forest we go,
To see all the big trees blow
The ponies and the deer are wandering,
At Buckler's hard river come to find a sanderling
And the birds are singing merrily, a picket post
Or roam to Barton-on-Sea by coast.
Athward the Oriental Drive is a sheer delight,
And of course the Knightwood Oak is a memorable sight.
A pace to Stoney Cross you may tumble on a wombat
Hurry down to Burley Green cricketer's shout 'Hows that!'
Rise up to Thorney Hill where the horses meet
All those wondrous places a traveller greets.

Michael Davis

EVERY HOUSE A SOMEBODY

Husband, have you seen my bag? 'Twas here, a moment ago,
I put it on the table, I'm positive that's so.
Inside's my glasses, keys and wallet
Card from the library, for a book by Ken Follet.
Oh Husband where ever is my bag?
Surely, you must know.

Husband have you seen my specs? They were upon the shelf,
I wore them when the vicar called, I did, I know, myself
Can't read the paper or watch TV.
Can't wipe the mud off Jimmy's knee,
Husband, have you seen my specs?
You must know where they are.

Husband have you seen my knickers? They were on the washing line!
That scrap of lace, they're Mary Ann's; the bigger ones are mine!
To the supermarket I need to go,
Wind's in the east, how it does blow.
Husband, have you seen my knickers?
It's draughty - down below!

There's a somebody in every house, surely, you'll agree,
Things go missing, goodness knows where, and all say ''Twas not me'
Theatre tickets, the village hall keys,
Letter from our boy, he's overseas.
There's a somebody in every house.
Could it just be - you!

Pamela Carder

SLIM CHANCE

I heard a very funny thing -
I wish I could remember -
It started with a silly ass
Whose birthday's in September.

September 10th, I think it is,
It doesn't really matter.
He wanted books on dieting
'Cause he was getting fatter.

His mates they tried so very hard,
Although they thought him barmy -
They bought a very pricey book
'The Thin Red Line' (the army).

His wife went even further
She bought a video, dammit
The film was called 'The Thin Man'
By a bloke called Dashiell Hammett.

A history buff was helpful
In his own peculiar terms,
He offered a lengthy treatise
Snappy title - 'Diet of Worms'.

The silly ass was very pleased
Although he was no thinner,
But everyone had tried so hard
He asked them all to dinner.

D M Anderson

DRUMOSSIE MOOR

In 1746
One cold and dismal day,
Geordie's redcoats came a'calling
They had a debt to pay.

The clans were there to meet them,
Footsore, starved and cold,
Honour bound with valiant hearts,
Warriors true and bold.

The eerie highland war cries,
Rang across the marsh,
Cannon barked their answer
Death came swift and harsh.

They fell among the heather,
All the moor was red,
English coats and highland blood,
Blending with the dead.

So by shades of evening,
Bonnie Charlie's men were done,
The English walked among them,
Dispensing comfort with a gun.

Starvation, hangings, torture,
Retribution filled with hate,
The English razed the highlands,
Left desolation in their wake.

And now it's only clan stones,
Mark those who've gone before,
Which stand as silent witness,
To the slaughter on the moor.

Helen Lloyd

SYDNEY THE SNAIL

Sydney the snail was lonely in life,
so he felt it was time he looked for a wife.
He set out one day determined to find
a snail who was lovely, gentle and kind.

He thought that his quest was certain to fail,
when he happened to meet his dream of a snail.
And so they were married early one dawn,
as overnight dew still lay on the lawn.

They set up home in the base of a shrub,
surrounded by flowers and plenty of grub.
And the lone life of Sydney was well in the past,
as now he was happy and contented at last.

So next time you see a silvery trail,
it was probably made by Sydney the snail.
While you were sleeping he was taking the chance,
of munching his way through all of your plants.

Helen T Westley

A GOOD TIME

A holiday should be a pleasure,
Two weeks of sunshine and much leisure,
Ours started badly the taxi was late,
And the plane had left sealing our fate.

At last on board a sigh of relief,
Short lived a large lady sat in the next seat,
'Oh' she squealed, 'isn't this topping'
As she squashed us with her bottom,
Worse was to come with no retreat.

At dinner she decided she wanted a curry,
Then said she felt sick, we tried to move in a hurry,
Too late we had to accept our fate,
So we reached the hotel soiled and a little bit late.

The manager asked for our cases and money
There was no cases 'Sorry Sonny,'
The cases had gone on the wrong plane,
Oh boy is it possible can we stay sane?

For two weeks we coped with only toothbrush and nightwear,
A change of clothes and the same footwear,
Back at the airport we thought we looked good,
Clean shorts, T-shirt and sunglasses to boot.

Customs said, 'Do you think we are mugs,'
'Open it up we think you've got drugs,'
Back on the aircraft, we sat very quiet,
Then the stewardess said, 'You're on the wrong flight.'

My wife then turned and said to me,
'What we need is a holiday, don't you agree?'
I collapsed in my seat with an almighty groan,
I told her, 'Never again, we're staying at home!'

Elizabeth Hiddleston

PADDY'S SURE THING!

There's a horse running Saturday
And it's a *sure thing!*
All I have to do
Is give *your man* a ring

Not to have bet
Why it would be a sin
Your man is normally right
So it will surely win

These were the words
That *Paddy* spoke
Deadly serious
It was no joke

A tenner I placed
Upon its nose
That Saturday
When I arose

'Sure Thing' set off
And out of sight
It must have had wings
As it took flight

Like a breeze
I saw it go past
A flight of fancy
It came in *last!*

David Duthie

NIPPED IN THE BUD

This is the sad tale of a sad niece who,
Whilst visiting, went to the loo,
But what a shock that poor girl got
When on the seat she put her bot,
The seat, all clean and shiny black,
In fact, was lurking for attack,
As hidden in its glossy rim,
There was a tiny crack within,
And as her broad posterior sat
Down on the seat, the little crack,
With eager jaws now open wide,
Just took a bite at her backside.

She simply could not up and run,
For a job's a job, and must be done,
To draw attention to her plight
With trousers down, did not seem right.
She simply had to grin and bear,
This outrage on her naked rear,
She lodged complaint, with eyes a-smarting,
Whilst we just fell about, a-laughing.
Now all is well, and danger gone,
A new seat's there to sit upon.
The old one, crack an' all departs,
On Wednesday, via the old dust cart.

The moral of this tale - be wise,
Watch where, and how, you sit and rise,
Don't trust those black and shiny plastics,
They may play bold with your elastics!

Joan Hammond

A PERFUMED GARDEN

We wound our way through the countryside
Through leafy lanes, so narrow - not wide
But steep and steeper still did we climb
'Til we came to garden so sublime
That lay past the pub at the top of the hill
The sight that met us gave us such a thrill
A garden walled with a mellow red brick
Enclosed a space - did our eyes play a trick?

As I looked around at the rows and rows
Of blooms which assailed my senses - my nose
Was filled with a fragrance so divine
That as I inhaled it - I felt it combine
And connect with my own inner wisdom
Oh, what a joy! Oh, what a kingdom!
Of vibrant colours so dazzling and bright
I could only dream of such pure delight

We joined a group, so friendly and eager
To learn of this plant - our knowledge was meagre
An hour was spent in utter bliss
I felt like giving the owner a kiss
At the end of the tour, we learnt to distil
The oil from this plant that can heal any ill
I came away with a loaded car
Filled to the brim with divine lavender.

Gina Bowman

GROWING OLD

Now I am old and grey,
Nobody comes my way,
Seems I have had my day,
Growing old.

Dreams that I thought would last,
Sadly, all in the past,
How did it go so fast?
Growing old.

Memories of yesterday,
Why do they fade away?
I don't know, I don't know.

There are tasks I still need to do,
Joys I still need to seek,
In my heart, still a dream or two,
But why does the flesh feel so weak?

Friends that I knew have gone,
Disappeared, one by one,
Glad we met, won't forget.

Spring and summer are memories now,
Autumn leaves turned to gold,
I'll survive winter's chill somehow,
And pray I go on, growing old.

I shouldn't feel sad,
I ought to be glad,
Still fun to be had,
I'm still here! Begad!
Growing old.

Jim Storr

THE HAM SANDWICH

I was in a deep discussion, with my mother-in-law
On the merit of a sandwich and other things galore!
Should the bread be sliced or unsliced? Thick, medium or thin?
Supermarket or bakery? With or without packaging?
Never use a loaf that is stale, because it's past its best!
A sandwich is 'par excellence' if you choose bread that's fresh!
We need to use a special knife, when cutting on a board.
If this is done correctly, the surface won't be scored!
Is it butter we require or is it low fat spread?
Remember to fully cover the corners of the bread!
As for our 'terminology' . . ! What is meant by 'a round'?
It's not as simple as you think! Variety, we found!

Cooked ham is lacking in appeal if it is covered in 'slime'!
And you really shouldn't wash it, but eat it in good time!
There is crumbed and honey-roast ham, ham-off-the-bone, as well!
Some are cheap, some are expensive, some are 'reduced to sell'!
To cut the fat off from the ham is a wise thing to do!
For the sandwich will be tasty and you'll be healthy, too!
Then a little pepper and salt, to enhance the flavour,
Maybe a touch of garnish, adding to the savour!
Finally, we cut the sandwich, such a creative art!
Halves, quarters, squares and triangles - all of an equal part!
The sandwiches are all arranged, in beauty, on a plate!
Alas, their beauty does not last - they can't avoid their *fate!*

Jenny Stevens

INTERFERENCE

He worked and worked so hard at school
and 'homeworked' every night
he did not want to seem a fool
though he really was quite bright.

His marks at school said he'd done well
· the masters he could trust
the 'A' level exams were hell
and that's when he went bust.

Although he thought he'd passed the lot
with all his grades an 'A'
from the ministry there'd come a clot
downgrading him that day.

His life was ruined from that time on
he lost his uni' place
'cause the moron who had 'flipped a coin'
had left him in disgrace.

On orders from the QCA
his work, for all to see,
was graded, not the truthful 'A'
but a nasty lying 'B'.

So all the hard, hard work he'd done
through 12 long years at school,
had been negated by a 'hun'
an interfering fool.

No years at 'U', no 'first' degree
although he'd done his bit
'twas all for naught for he'd been caught
by a loathsome 'jobsworth' twit.

This last word can be changed around
by anyone with wit
'twould rhyme the same if it were found
to read 'unfit', 'git', 's**t'.

D G W Garde

UNTITLED

There was a young lady from Reading
Who found that her waistline was spreading
She said with a moan
'I've put on half a stone
My next Weight Watchers weigh-in I'm dreading.'

Marjorie Grant

CELESTE

Gentle as a warm summer's breeze;
Blue eyes bright as a springtime morn.
Such beauty that cold hearts unfreeze;
Her smile like a wonderful dawn.

Intelligent, compassionate,
Tearful when hearing children sing;
Sentimental, affectionate;
Makes a man feel like a king.

I wish I'd met her years ago
But then she would have been quite young
And I an ageing Romeo
Reaching life's ladder's middle rung.

From Latin is her middle name,
Caelestis 'heavenly' Celeste;
Being near her is just the same
As a feeling divinely blessed.

I love her so very dearly;
Life can be cruel; such is fate.
Alas I was born too early
And sadly she was born too late.

William Barnard

A LOVE THAT

A love that never dies
A love with no lies
A love that feels right
A love that doesn't keep you awake at night
A love that feels nice
A love that doesn't pay a price
A love where you both can try
A love that doesn't live a lie
A love that grows deep in your heart
A love that doesn't tear you apart
A love that you can feel the romance between you
A love that feels right in everything you do
That's all I ask for
I don't ask for more.

Marc P Weaver

WITH LOVE TO MY SONS

In the year 2000 I lost after 50 years
A person so loving and very dear
He was the love of my life
I now miss him day and night

My sons with families of their own
All now fully grown
Have been my help and loving sons
Never leaving a thing undone

To help me through this loss
Which I have never counted the cost
I have never really expressed my thanks
To these lads who have never broken ranks

The help they have given me
Has helped me through my loss you see
So how do you thank so much devotion?
I do not have any notion

So thank you my lovely sons
For everything you have done
To help me get over this loss
I can imagine what it has cost.

Jean Bradbury

GHOSTLY RECOLLECTIONS

I am sure I have walked these streets before
In a previous life sometime
I can recognise every painted door
And the lattice windows edged with grime

The scent of flowers seems so familiar
As I linger in this wood
It reminds me of a distant age
Yet, this is where I stood

This hotel was once a meeting place
For the infamous and rich
And still I can smell the plain cuisine
Amongst the salt and pitch

Fashion and standards have changed with time
But the music still sounds clear
This is the 21st century
But I swear I once stood here.

Lynda Fordham

THE SCARECROW AND THE BLACKBIRD

I saw a scarecrow in a field,
His eyes were two green peas.
His nose - a carrot,
And his mouth - a smiling slice of cheese!
His purpose was to keep away
Birds of every size!
But when a blackbird came along
He liked those pea-green eyes.
He pecked at one and then the next,
His breakfast was complete,
By lunchtime he was hungry,
So returned to have a treat.
The carrot looked inviting,
So did the smiling cheese,
But while he was deciding
A worm crept up the sleeve
Of Sam the scarecrow's jacket;
The blackbird had to choose
Protein, cheese or carrot?
He nearly blew a fuse!
When Sam the scarecrow gave a sneeze
And lost his mouth and nose!
The worm just squirmed in fear, because
He really had supposed
He'd be next on the menu;
But the blackbird had turned white,
'A-tishoo!' was his song at dawn
His virus - scarecrow fright!

Marion Skelton

ELVIS

Elvis was king, he used to sing everything,
soul, gospel, blues, even rock 'n' roll.
He used to wiggle his hips and tap his feet
from his heels to his toes.
You were taken from your fans many years ago,
so God bless Elvis, keep on rocking,
in that great big blue yonder in the sky,
because you will always be King.

D Hall

YESTERYEAR

As I took a stroll along the lane where you lived
The autumn leaves rustled and whispered beneath my feet
The memories of yesteryear stirred within my mind
As I passed the places where we used to meet

Those long ago glorious summer days and nights
When the world belonged to us, and to us alone
As we walked arm in arm through quiet leafy lanes
Listening to the breeze and its low haunting moan

I remembered the time that you came into my life
Like the kiss of a small drop of rain
As it brushed on a leaf and fell gently down
To refresh the parched earth once again

You were a nocturne in a musical wilderness
You were the nectar of a wild summer rose
You were warm, you were sweet, you were gentle
I could never forget such memories as those

And now as I walk along the lane where you lived
In the late autumn's fast falling light
I must fade away, like the rays of each sun
Like a tall ship that has passed in the night.

Derek Bradley

THE TYPICAL MAN
(Dedicated to my dad, William John Charles Knightly Jnr)

He drinks from the carton
He leaves up the seat
The typical man
That most people meet

He brings you flowers
And chocolates galore
The type of man
That women want more

Tall, dark and handsome
Oh, you're kidding me
They're as rare as the dodo
But they aren't stingy

Really now
Are men good or bad?
Well my typical man
Is a dude I call Dad

Yes, he's one weird guy
But he fits all of the above
Yes, he's my dad
Who I love.

Laura Knightly

I DON'T LIKE CARROTS

Down by the railway cutting were allotments by the score,
'The Association' owned them, and also many more;
my father a keen gardener, vegetables he would grow
the biggest and the best were Dad's, from onions to marrow.

He would enter competitions with everything he'd got
and walk away with prizes - most times he'd take the lot,
but no one knew the secret of the flavour and the size
he said he hadn't got one, and Dad did not tell lies.

We ate carrots, sprouts and cabbage, parsnips, beans and beet,
our plates were piled with all of this and very little meat,
the flavour always was superb 'Dad - where's your secret hid?'
'I only plant and pray' he said, 'the rest the good Lord did.'

One day, when on our way to play we passed Dad's Holy ground,
and saw the local dogs were out for their morning run-around;
up and down the rows they went and stopped occasionally
to lift their little furry legs, on the carrots - not a tree.

His secret stayed with us for years until we reached our teens
and no one ever really knew why we all went off our greens.
So when I see a carrot or a parsnip, at a horticulture show -
I wonder if the doggies helped to make those vegetables grow.

Jim Pritchard

DARTMOOR DAWN

Night shadow in the vale,
full moon bathes the hill,
fresh dew on my feet
keen breeze gives a chill.

From the peak of Sharp Tor
the horizon is red,
as the orb breaks through
a new dawn is shed.

The sky seems on fire,
in the splendour I drown,
ancient granite surrounds me
and sheep graze the down.

Soon the rays become warm,
moist rocks and heather shine bright,
gorse flowers start to twinkle,
so refreshing . . . sunlight.

Bill Breton

GOLDILOCKS RETURNS

Once upon a time
There was a little bear.
He heard a knocking on his door.
So he yelled out, 'Who is there?'
'Goldilocks,' a voice replied.
'I was sleeping in your bed.
I was frightened when awoken.
So when I saw you, I just fled.
I've now returned to your lovely home
And I would like to mend your chair,
I've brought with me some porridge oats
Enough for all to share.
Where's your mum and where's your dad
I've got the porridge in the pot.
You'd better go and find them
While the porridge is still hot.'
Little bear told Mum and Dad
While picking berries for to eat,
'Goldilocks has cooked some oats
And also fixed my seat.'
Mum and Dad said, 'Let's go home
While the porridge is still hot.'
So they all sat down together
And ate the very lot.

Stephen Hibbeler

IN HEAVEN'S SWEET WAYS

We all love our mother, it has to be said
But what do we do once she is dead?
The pain in our hearts, the loss oh so great
We're suddenly missing our dearest mate
Who can we run to when life is unfair?
It's horrible knowing that she's not there
Who to depend on when things go wrong
That beautiful face for whom we all long
To smile at our tears and make things go right
To help us all through life's long hard fight
The one that comforts us through thick and thin
The one that steers us away from sin
The wonderful loving arms that surround
Us with the tenderness and care to abound
The gentle hands that nurse and caress
All of our ails through falls and illness
She's one of the most precious gifts of all
Only now she's not here to answer our call
But we're so glad we had her for all of those years
And now we must strive on to have faith like hers
To carry us through to the end of our days
In hope that we'll meet her in Heaven's sweet ways.

Caroline Kelsey

Everlasting Friends

Others drift quietly, on a summer's breeze,
Some blow violently, through winter's trees.
Others go, with a gentle weep,
Some go, with a cheery cheek.
Others we hold, in a warm embrace,
Some we smack, and then displace.
Many have gone, and have disappeared,
And the ones who stay, who won't run, or flee,
Are those people, we call family.

S S Jackson

SUNDAY'S MYSTERY TOUR

Travelling away from familiar places
Beyond the realms of the great Prince Bishops
This road is bumpy and round it curves
Into different scenes as we get under way
Warmed by the sweltering heat of this hot day.
Sun, shade, sun, some coolness felt
Beneath sharp flashes from fleeting woody trees.
The open windows in our stifling bus
Allowing quick draughts to blow our hair.
Through quaint villages we ride on -
Stokesley, stopping, to wander through
Village shops, waiting in village streets, tea rooms.
On again through majestic mountains, growing trees
Turning swerved roads, more scenery comes to the eye.
Cattle and sheep, grazing fields
Rabbits run, chickens peck
A sparrow hawk hovers the sky.
Pheasant and young on the road ahead
Our bus slows down to let them safely over
Watching adults and children ooh and aah,
Young scurry, the pheasant stops
Standing to see that all young have crossed.
Road signs tell us of our mystery destination
Aching feet as we wander round the sights of Whitby.
Back to the bus, this hot afternoon travels bright and on
The glaring sun warming up the colours
Of purple heathers and sun-baked brackens
Passing fir trees, wooded copses, Yorkshire's passion,
Yachts skim over glistening waters of Scaling reservoir
Over and down the steep gradient of Sutton bank,
Engine running, wheels turning onto Cleveland.
Back to busy streets, traffic lights and houses.

People quiet, as dusk changes the scene around us.
'B' roads, lead us back to familiar surroundings
On into County Durham, and home.
To ponder on, and write of what was seen.

Susan Carole Roberts

TEETH

Grandad has teeth and he takes them out
His mouth looks really funny.
I have tried to take mine out
Cos Grandad gives me money.
Said that I could look like him
Just two rows of gums,
And though I am young
And mine stay in
Just wait till old age comes!

Margaret Carter

BLISS

A frightened old shadow hid out of sight
Its master had died late last night
He knew that a shadow must never be seen
Without the person that once had been
Sadly thinking back on so many happy years
It was now time to leave his home
And brushed away the tears.
Waiting till the quiet of the midnight hour
The old shadow summoned his fading power
Then slowly started walking down the stair
Such a strange feeling with the master not there
Almost now to the last bottom step then
He had to stride over old faithful sleeping Shep
Now along the corridor nearly to the hall door
When a beautiful shadow appeared
Of the one who had gone before.
They merged together in a lingering kiss
And slowly disappeared, into a shadowy bliss.

H J Mazza

UNTITLED

The day we went on holiday
On Boeing's silver bird
Became a day we'd not forget
A drama quite absurd.

At check-in desk the girl severe
Viewed tickets, passports too
Pack these yourself? No bombs? She asked
Before she'd let us through.

The cases then she weighed and tagged
And sent them on their way
To where? And if we'd see them soon
We really couldn't say.

You'll see them when you reach Beijing
There didn't seem much chance,
Whilst we flew off to far Cathay
Our undies went to France.

We never saw our clothes again
And though we made our claim
To have to dress as Chinese do
Was really not the same!

Norman Woosey

THE NEW YEAR

Christmas is over, and thank God for that!
The meals prepared, eaten and supped,
Gone are the blues from a hangover before,
Mopping the blood, sweat and tears from the floor!

Now the New Year, equally a bore,
With cold roast chicken, only the cat wants more!
The mistletoe curling, long past its day,
Leaving all who enter, in a daze.

Feeling limp, the hour is here,
For those who wish to celebrate the New Year,
Listening in for the bells to toll,
As others decide to take a stroll.

The morning after, just look at the floor,
With wasted peanuts, mince pies, and more,
Often with a headache with the anticlimax to show,
Just how the season is left, I really don't know!

On the twelfth night, the cards come down,
Often with a rain of dust, as we frown,
Thank God for that, we all sigh with relief,
No more of that for 353 days, good grief!

Rosemary E Pearson

I SAW YOU

I saw you smile,
I saw you cry,
and all the while
I would sit and sigh.

I saw you laugh,
I saw you frown
at the wedding photograph
I would always move around.

I saw you stare
at winter's bitter ice,
and bad times did recur
to make life, not so nice.

I saw you in all seasons
look, with those starry eyes,
so there are many, many reasons
why I love you, I hope you realise.

I saw you look at moonbeams,
and ponder deep at oceans blue,
I'm glad I was in your many dreams,
thanks for letting me, love you!

Tony Heenan

THE GRANDMOTHER CLOCK

Thinking back to when, I was a kid
My sister and I, and the things we did
Picking Grandma's raspberries, for a pie
Out wriggled maggots, I thought I'd die.

But my sister laughed, teased, and thought it fun
And threw them at me, if I didn't run.
In school holidays; we'd go and spot the trains
We'd always say it didn't matter, if it rains.

Fairs and circuses, clowns and chimps
A day at the seaside, hunting crabs and shrimps
Good times then at three pennies a ride
But our sandcastles got ruined by the tide

Childhood days, soon turned to romance
I met my other half, at a dance
The kids arrived and made us happy
But I'll never forget, the terry nappy.

We had to work to pay the bills
And got colds, the sniffles, and other ills
A day trip, or Butlins year after year
Good and bad times, sometimes a tear.

Looking in the mirror now, I know I'm the granny
With six different voices all shouting 'Nanny'
But the clock keeps on ticking in a different way
Computers and tele, replace the games we'd play.

But the excitement of Christmas will always stay
With Granny and Grandad's presents on Christmas Day
But time doesn't stop, and one day you'll be
A granny, like my granny and *me.*

Mary McNulty

WILDLIFE TALES OF HYLTON CASTLE
CROSSING THE A19 ROAD

The night was dark and damp, the ground soft with falling rain,
Spike the hedgehog stood at the side of the A19
Scratching his head, he racked his brain
Thinking aloud he thought, 'How can I cross this road tonight
So that I'm safely home with my family at first light?'
The traffic was heavy and moved very fast
Each vehicle snarling loudly as it roared past
Caused Spike to think this night would be his last.

Just then a gentle voice said, 'Hello Spike, what ails you, this night?'
And Spike saw his friend Robbie Rabbit,
In the light of the car's headlights
'Why Robbie,' said Spike, 'it's nice to see you my dear friend,
But I'm on this side of the road, and my house is at the other end.'
'That's no great problem Spike, my dear friend,' Robbie replied
'Come with me, and I'll soon get you to the other side.'
And so to Robbie's burrow, Spike was quickly shown
Then under the A19 and in safety he reached home.

Snug as a bug and safely home, he told his wife the tale that night
For he believed Robbie Rabbit had saved his life,
Next day to Robbie's home, Spike again made his way,
And thanked Robbie for allowing him to see the light of day
'Spike,' said Robbie, 'that's what friends are for.
You'd have done the same for me, and more I'm sure.'
And so began the friendship of Robbie and Spike that night,
One that carried them through many adventures of life.

R Marr

I DREAM

I dream this world could be a better place,
Somewhere to live no matter what your race.
There is so much violence in the world today,
I dream it may get better someday.
So much hurt, so much pain,
There really isn't much to gain.
But people say some dreams come true,
Well fingers crossed it's all down to you.
So no matter what race you are,
Enjoy your life you have only *one*.

Carol Coker

Not Very Well

Don't ask the man how he's feeling,
He'll give it you chapter and verse.
You may think you are helping the healing.
You'll finish by making it worse.

For he likes to recount every minute,
Each snuffle and snivel and sneeze.
If there was a prize he would win it.
For describing his cough and his wheeze.

He thinks he looks rough and rejected.
He does, but I wouldn't dare say.
He's feeling so down and dejected.
His nose has been running all day.

He's using up acres of tissue,
He's sighing all over the place.
His nose is becoming an issue,
Beginning to glow on his face.

He'll complain, with incredible anguish,
There's nothing at all he can do.
He just wants to lie there and languish.
Relying completely on you.

In this he'll be utterly ruthless,
For whether he's young or he's old.
There is no one so utterly useless,
As the man who's enjoying a cold.

Dave Deakin

YOU ARE EVERYTHING

I look to what makes me tick
It is my heart
Darling it is you
My other part.
What makes me smile and wink
Concentrate and think
To go ahead.
It is my brain
And Sweetheart it is you again
When we walk hand in hand
Life becomes grand
Put up our feet
We rest our weary limbs
Life cycle is complete.

Allan John Mapstone

THOUGHTS OF MY MOTHER

Her life was long, yet wearisome - with pain and grief so rife
Yet happy days and pleasant ways - lightened her skein of life.
I know I caused her heartache which went on to cause more pain
Too late to say 'If only' and 'I'd not do that again'.
She'd so much beauty in her yet my eyes did fail to see
How blind my heart to all the love she daily offered me.
All through her life she loved the sun and revelled in its heat
A garden was her fav'rite spot - amongst the flowers sweet.
Tenaciously she clung to life - she did not want to leave
For her three children left behind - she knew how we would grieve.
And so a letter she arranged - to read when she had left,
To let us know she loved us so - and not to feel bereft.
She wrote 'When day is over and you come to take your ease.
When sitting in your gardens and you feel the kiss of breeze.
Then when you feel the warmth of sun fall gently on your hair
It is my fingers that you feel. You'll know that I am there'.
But all our faults and failings we know she will truly pardon
And love us while she takes her rest in God's eternal garden.

Pamela R Dalton

A DOGGY TALE

The dog was lost - what could he do?
Who could he go running to?
Lost and hungry he wandered around,
Then suddenly someone was there - he was found!
He was taken to a place where lost dogs go,
With lots of others he didn't know.
He was fed and watered but locked in a cage,
Some of the dogs got into quite a rage.
People came round and looked them over,
But they didn't want one that was a Rover.
Until one day a family came to see
Which dog they would like in the family.
He tried to give them a word to the wise
By pleading with his gentle eyes.
Please take me - I'm the one you need,
He used everything he had to plead.
The family fell for him straight away
And took him home that very day.
You may ask me how I know -
Because my grandchildren told me so!

J Evans

A MESSAGE

You're here for a reason
You're here for a season

Just for a moment, push everything aside
Just for a moment, forget about pride
Open your heart, set your mind free
Become, you, the person you are meant to be.

You're here for a reason
You're here for a season

So recognise your purpose, don't dwell on your mistakes
God chose you for greatness, so go on, be great
And just for a moment, forget troubles, hurts and strifes
Now take that moment and begin the rest of your life.

Gladys Lawson

A FRIEND INDEED

Living alone through twilight years
Sadly harassed by inner fears
Resolutely resisting pangs of despair
Then a tiny puppy answered a prayer

Playful as a little child
Boisterous and running wild
Gradually mellowing as she grew
Constantly learning something new

Wakes each morning full of zest
Surely understands every request
Fetches her lead, then begs
Eager to stretch those four legs

Bounding off across the park
Innocently providing a vital spark
Tireless energy and exuberant extremes
Recalling happy childhood dreams

Lovingly cherished, kept warm and fed
Always knows when it's time for bed
A comfortable basket on the floor
No cause to worry anymore

Though it's lonely without a spouse
She has transformed the house
Faithfully filling every need
Having found a friend indeed.

A W Day

PROGRESSION OR REGRESSION?

The rainforest is going faster, than we would hope.
Rare breeds, rare plants, and medicines to help us cope.
The car, a product of our so called intelligent invention,
Burning fuel, polluting the air, with destructive intention.
Black or white, or in-between, the colours of our skin.
Religion, nationality, what really matters is what's within.
We should have learned from wars of past years,
The hatred between one man and another man's fears.
Have we progressed? Yes, with hate and jeers.
Basic living, simple tasks, a world of tears.

Sue Jenkins

BUTTON CONFUSION

We have videos and DVDs
Music tapes and also CDs,
Computers that drive us to distraction,
I wish I knew how to get in on the action,
We have all these handsets lined up in a row.
Which one to pick up I just do not know,
With so many buttons to press and to choose,
I wish I could lose them as I get so confused,
Then there are tapes which are piled up high,
If we put them together they would reach to the sky,
'It has something on it, so don't use that tape,'
But is it a film or just a debate?
'Will we ever find out,' I say with a grin,
As we are always too tired, or we're out and not in,
Then there is short play or long play to double,
If we don't watch some soon there will be some trouble,
We will buy some new shelves to get tapes off the floor,
That will give us some space then we can buy more,
For any more gadgets we have no more room,
The way things are going we will have to move soon,
In this day and age everything is so fast,
I'll try to get used to it but I know it won't last,
Can't we slow the pace down,
So we all aren't so stressed?
Soon we will realise it is for the best,
Just give me a knob and a dial I can see,
It might not please everyone,
But it would certainly please *me!*

Elsie Kemp

MY SUNDAY BOY

The child that is born on the Sabbath day
Is bonnie and blithe and good and gay,
And my Sunday boy was no exception
With beguiling green eyes and fresh complexion.

Blithe and gay he was in all sorts of ways;
His infectious laughter would our spirits raise.
Most times, as the rhyme says, he was good,
But he was quite naughty if in that mood.

Now he is a man with his own family,
A lovely wife and children three,
But he is still my bonnie Sunday boy,
And along with his sister, my pride and joy.

Marlene Allen

PRESENT ABSENCE

'I will love you till I die'.
I declared this to the sky
When your fax arrived today
Stating clearly that you may
Catch a plane to bring you home,
From your business trip to Rome,
Tuesday next if not before.
Why you go I am not sure.
Surely you could use the phone,
Then I'd not be left alone.
Yet it's when we are apart
Thoughts of you invade my heart,
Allowing love to be restored
All the time you are abroad.

Henry Disney

THOMAS KITTEN

Thomas kitten awoke one day,
And said to himself, I'll go out to play,
He went to find his saucer of milk,
And cleaned his coat till it shone like silk.

Out in the garden he found a mouse . . .
Chased it around, then it ran in the house,
Mum came and found them chasing about
And said, 'You are naughty, go on out.'

While he was not looking, the mouse ran away,
So Tom thought it was time to call it a day,
Mum had put supper in his dish,
His favourite tonight, oh good it was *fish*.

Betty Mason

SUNNY HOPES

I hope for a summer that's nice and hot
I've put up my tent - and it's there to stop.
Posh carpets now upon the floor,
Table, chairs and lots, lots more.
The barbecue's ready - we're all set to go
It depends on the weather as to how it will go
Please God I ask that the sun will shine
I don't mind a shower - that would be fine
But some sun would be nice
To show off my tent - then I could tell folk
It was heaven sent!

Janet Mary Kirkland

OWT FOR NOWT

'If tha does owt for nowt, mi lad, then do it for thissen,'
This strong advice did John receive, when at the age of ten.
He heeded it from day to day, thinking of number one,
Advantage for himself he sought, in this was all his fun.
When others he could see in need, however much their plight,
He was inclined to think and say, 'Blow you Jack, I'm alright.'
One day, he caused an accident, when out upon his bike.
His rival he was racing past, another boy called Mike.
Both lads were laid in the same ward, a broken leg had each,
An experience was this for John, did him a lesson teach.
Directly opposite lay Mike, had visits more and more.
How very many friends had he, but all did John ignore.
So, John was clearly not alright, the situation grim.
He later had one visitor, a boy whose name was Jim.
This fellow, whom he scarcely knew, what prompted him to call?
Jim told him that the news he'd heard, the broken leg and all,
In that same place, some time ago, had he been for a spell.
How well he knew what visits meant, so came to wish him well.
When hospital he duly left, John was glad to be whole
And in his teenage years he found, in life a different goal,
Apology he made, to Mike and thanks to Jim did give,
New friendships did he find with both, a better way to live.
A change had come about in him, gone were his selfish ways,
To younger boys, he'd give advice, learnt from his own sick days.
'If tha does owt for nowt, mi lad, tha'll get back more thissen.
Tha'll make a lot of friends that way, be 'appy once again.'

D J Price

CHRISTMAS

I love the hustle and bustle of Christmas preparations galore,
Buying and wrapping presents and cards,
Putting 'Welcome - Merry Christmas' on the door.
It's friends and neighbours time of year
For parties and gatherings of families dear,
With chains and tinsel sparkling so bright,
The tree decorated, baubles and colours - what a sight.
Santa peeping through branches and fairy with shiny wand above
A model of the manger on the sideboard reminding us all of Jesus' love
This is the time for children with dollies and games in parcels on high,
Waiting for the magical morning when Santa's had
                         his milk and mince pie.
We all love to sing the carols when we go to mass at midnight.
As we attend the service in glowing candlelight.
Christmas roast dinner is enjoyed by the crowd
The pudding, mince pies and fruit do us proud.
Then it's feet up to watch TV's speech by the Queen
With children trying out new toys - really keen.
It's soon time to sleep after the exciting day,
'God bless and Happy Christmas' as we go on our way.

Betty Lloyd

GRANDAD'S FEUD

Yellow and orange, below blue skies,
Nasturtiums share the summer day
With humming bees, while butterflies,
White-winged, flutter the hours away.

A different scene their flight recalls;
Long ago, in another place,
In a garden with high flint walls,
A sturdy grandad starts a chase.

'Those dratted, greedy cabbage whites!
Pretty butterflies! I'll be blowed!'
He cries, and eagerly he fights,
In portly pursuit and gallant mode.

A tennis racquet for his sword,
He drives and slashes, low and high,
And sometimes, for a just reward,
Impales a hapless butterfly.

A weighty faun, puffing, grunting,
Almost leaping, as to and fro
His racquet swings, fiercely hunting,
No quarter given to the foe!

At last, red-faced and out of breath,
He goes. The rest dance undeterred.
Perhaps it was a quicker death
Than being gobbled by a bird!

It's true - as true as true can be.
I saw him then, with my own eyes.
My little sister came with me,
And watched our grandad with surprise.

Now, back beside my golden flowers,
I smile to think of those charmed hours.

Margaret Ballard

IT WOULD BE NICE

With flowers now bursting into bloom
Why is it there is so much gloom?
Is it because people are out of work and without pay?
And it is getting worse each passing day,
Why does it go on and who is to blame?
For this terrible waste and crying shame?
For all those people who only want to work
And not because of any work that they shirk,
They who want to get out of the lowly gutter
And provide again their families with bread and butter,
Will it all come back ever again?
Our factories full of work and out to make a gain,
It would be nice if we were again blooming
And once again the people's families consuming,
So let us hope it all gets better soon
Before they all off to the moon.

George W Reed

My Day To Remember

From a land of dreams I opened my eyes,
Through a sky of blue shone a brilliant sunrise,
A summer day to remember it was going to be
The rise and shine message I obeyed immediately.

From Birmingham's noisy city I was up and away
To the peace of the countryside to Wales for one day
Discovering hills and valleys nature's beauty to see,
Along quiet country roads feeling uplifted and free.

No frustrating hold-ups or long stressful queues
Bathed in sunshine, relaxed, absorbed picturesque views.
Contented cows quietly munching in rich fields of green
White sheep dotted on hillsides, busy farmsteads seen.

In fields standing silently black rolls covered hay,
Farmers with machines completed a hay-making day.
Noticed 'Rosy apples, fresh veg and potatoes for sale'
Was a good year for farmers when crops did not fail.

Green hops in fields in long rows climbing tall
'Local cider for sale' good country drink for all.
Trees in crowded orchards, heavy with fruit at its best
Nature's late summer fulfilment for its 2002 harvest.

Yonder on far distant hills, fields of green, brown and gold
Formed a pretty patchwork pattern so colourful to behold.
Visions of slowly gliding shadows over hills by cloud and sun
Shining in the sky of blue sending its warmth to everyone.

Down leafy country lanes with many a winding bend
Flickering sunlight filtered through dancing sunbeams it did send.
Oh! The magic of the countryside where sparkling streams flow
Everything is alive and wonderful and nature says 'Grow, grow'.

Historical village in the valley, timbered houses black and white,
Colourful hanging baskets, pretty cottage post office in sight
A quaint 'Running Horse' pub, church and cemetery for folk gone,
Do hope my day to remember, has enthralled everyone.

Stella Bush-Payne

IF YOU BELIEVE

I share, I sure do
My love and dreams
My faith and dreams
My hope and dreams
    From many towns
    From many cities
    From many kingdoms
    From many, many, many realms.

Put my trust in love
Put my dreams in love
Put my mercy in love
Put my stake in love

And we all sang a song
And we all sang a song.

If you believe
    Truth never turns a blind eye
Oh Lord! Truth never
Oh Lord! Truth never
Oh Lord! Truth never turns a blind eye
    But in an instant
    It can make you blush
    It can make you cry.

Paul Davidson

CHALKIE'S HORSE

Chalkie loved his little horse
The best friend he'd ever had
Just like part of the family
He thought Chalkie was his dad

You would always see Chalkie
With his companion Dobbin
Totally inseparable
Like Batman and just Robin

Chalkie would dine with Dobbin
While sitting in the stables
He preferred to eat indoors
But horses won't sit at tables

Now horses don't live forever
One day you are bound to cry
Because he has gone to graze
On those pastures in the sky

He spent all his time with Dobbin
To avoid his nagging wife
So when the horse dropped dead
It completely changed his life

'I wish it was her who'd died,'
He said speaking from the heart
'Her dung's no good for gardens
And she couldn't pull the cart.'

Tedward

FEELING THE HEAT (OR COLD)?

Older people feel the cold
So we're told.
Not me, just 83

When summer comes I dread hot, sunny days
Blood pressure rises, come dizzy spells
In many ways I suffer still
First felt in youth, I feel quite ill

Friends find it hard to understand my oddity

In winter they wish I'd wrap up more
What a bore
To try and cover up
To suffer more

Decency dictates however hot,
Streaking's taboo
The question is 'What can I do
But try explain my oddity?

Dolly Harmer

THE RISK

Had I the power to grant your aspirations,
Wishes, wakeful dreams or passing whim,
Your floating castles would be firmly planted
And the bubbles from your pipe all coloured in.

I'd tip the scales of life to show you favour,
Would iron out the worry from your brow
Then steer your destinations fast towards you
So you could make the most of 'here and now'.

Perhaps you'd then sail off into the sunset,
All laden with ambitions brave and new,
While I might sit reflecting, in my sorrow,
The fool I'd been to help your dreams come true!

Brenda Mentha

REPRIEVE

He'd stood there in front of the judge
The evidence against him he couldn't budge
Then the judge said without raising his head
'You'll hang by the neck until you're dead.'

So he sat there in his lonely cell
Nought could be heard but the sound of a bell
'Twas outside the prison in a solitary tower
And it rang out each and every hour.

The warder muttered 'Your time is nigh
See - yonder noose is swinging high,'
The prisoner gazed through the bars of his cell
Then he heard the sound of the bell.

The clock was striking the hour of seven
Its big hand was pointing up to Heaven
The bell was sounding out his knell
For surely now he was heading for Hell.

The cell door rattled and a priest stood there
He came and sat on the only chair
'I've come to say a prayer my Son
To forgive you for what you've done.'

'I didn't do it, Father,' he said
'If I'm to hang - be it on your head
I wasn't there when the woman died
Why should I lie - I've nothing to hide.'

They walked out into the morning light
The dangling noose was not a pretty sight
Around his neck they slid the noose
It lay there coiled - soft and loose.

Just then from the prison came a shout
One of the warders came rushing out
'I've got some news you won't believe
The governor rang - you've got a reprieve.'

So they led him back to his lonely cell
Where there was no sound 'cept the sound of the bell
Maybe to Hell he wasn't bound
Whilst a ray of hope was still around.

Trevor Headley

THE CIRCLE

The ever reaching shore, its beauty refined
In nature's circle, its position defined.
The ocean's anvil, all these days
With stoical indifference, it stays.

Compared to this, our lives are but fleeting,
Our fate is nature's earthly meeting
In the end we are not so clever,
As only the rocks live forever.

Brett Lovett

ROSES

What flower could smell so sweet?
A scented bowl at Caesar's feet.
A lover's gift, to heal a rift,
A token, silent, love unspoken.
A panacea for hearts all broken.
The poet's foil, a gift, a token,
A thorny stem, to beauty unequalled
The placid white and fiery red,
A Valentine's gift, a lover's bed.
Evokes the lover, the lyricist too,
A message of love from me to you.

Graham Law

A KNIGHT'S TALE

One day the knights of old
All had a very bad cold
And called upon their mummies to help them,
But instead they all did get
Something they did not expect
As the mummies that came couldn't sort out phlegm.

The mummies were dead
And were underfed
And were covered in lots of long cloths
The knights, they did fear
What they could not hear
But the mummies did only fear moths.

Still there was a battle
That spooked lots of cattle
But in the end the mummies went home
The knights had all won
But each called their mum
And they gave them a ring on the phone.

The evil was gone
So they all sat upon
Their mummies' knees to feel good
The moral is much
It's to keep in touch
And so the lot of us should.

Camillia Zedan